O9-BTO-536

First Facts™

Learning about Money

Supply and Demand

by Janeen R. Adil

Consultant:
Sharon M. Danes, PhD
Professor and Family Economist
University of Minnesota

Capstone press

Mankato, Minnesota

First Facts is published by Capstone Press,
151 Good Counsel Drive, P.O. Box 669, Mankato, Minnesota 56002.
www.capstonepress.com

Library of Congress Cataloging-in-Publication Data
Adil, Janeen R.
    Supply and demand / by Janeen R. Adil.
    p. cm. — (First facts. Learning about money)
    Summary: "Introduces supply and demand and explains how supply and demand affect the
prices of things people buy"—Provided by publisher.
    Includes bibliographical references and index.
    ISBN-13: 978-0-7368-5397-2 (hardcover)
    ISBN-10: 0-7368-5397-9 (hardcover)
    1. Supply and demand—Juvenile literature. 2. Prices—Juvenile literature. I. Title. II. Series.
HB801.A29 2006
338.5'21—dc22   2005020623

Editorial Credits
Wendy Dieker, editor; Jennifer Bergstrom, set designer; Bobbi J. Dey, book designer;
    Jo Miller, photo researcher/photo editor

Photo Credits
AP Wide World Photos/Charles Rex Arbogast, 11; Wilfredo Lee, 5
Capstone Press/Karon Dubke, cover, 6, 7, 10, 12–13, 14, 15, 16–17, 19, 21
Getty Images Inc./Tim Boyle, 8–9
Index Stock Imagery/Photolibrary.com, 20

Capstone Press thanks Ray's Market in North Mankato, Minnesota, for their help
in preparing this book.

Table of Contents

What Is Supply and Demand?

Have you ever really wanted something? And at the store, did you have to stand in line to get it? You were learning about supply and demand.

Supply is the **amount** of **goods** and **services** there are to buy. Demand is how many people want to buy those goods and services.

Fun Fact!
People who shop right before Christmas often find long lines at stores that sell popular toys.

Big Supply, Small Supply

Supply can be big, small, or in between. A big supply means many **choices** or a large amount. Jacob can choose any of these kinds of cereal.

A small supply means few choices or a small amount. Andrew takes the last piece of cheese pizza. The small supply has run out.

Demand

Demand can be high or low. Many kids want the new Harry Potter book. It has high demand. Only a few kids want the old Harry Potter book. That book has low demand.

Fun Fact!

Harry Potter and the Half-Blood Prince is the fastest selling book, with 8.9 million copies sold in 24 hours.

Double Play
2 packs
for
$1.99 + tax

Limited Edition!
Numbered
Johnny Bench
$15.00 + tax

Prices

Sometimes items have a small supply and high demand. People are willing to pay more money for these rare items.

Other times, items have a big supply and a low demand. Stores have to lower the **price**. More people will buy those items if they cost less money.

Too Many Choices

Sometimes **customers** have too many choices. Thousands of places sell pizza. The supply of sellers is big.

Some pizza places will lower their prices to get customers. Molly picks the place that sells pizza for less than the others.

> **Fun Fact!**
> The United States has over 60,000 pizza places. That's a big supply of sellers!

Not Enough Choices

At the movies, only one stand
sells popcorn. The supply of sellers is
small. But the demand is still high. The
popcorn stand can charge a high price.

Kyle and Jenny are hungry for hot popcorn. They pay a high price because they can't get popcorn anywhere else at the movies.

Mr. Wong's Bakery

Mr. Wong has a bakery. Every day, he bakes many loaves of bread. Most days, he sells all of the bread. Mr. Wong's customers think he has a fair price. He has a **balance** between supply and demand.

Fun Fact!
Two loaves of bread might seem like a small supply. But if only two people want bread, it is just right.

Lower Demand, Lower Price

Some days, Mr. Wong doesn't sell all his fresh bread. He sells that bread the next day. The demand for day-old bread is lower than for fresh bread. Mr. Wong lowers the price of day-old bread. Supply and demand make the prices change in Mr. Wong's bakery.

Fun Fact!

Balancing supply and demand helps avoid waste. Grocery stores have a good balance. They throw away only 1 percent of their food.

> Friendly service
> Fresh products
> Fantastic prices

In-Store Special

OOps!
We made
too Much!
99¢
Day-Old
items

99¢

Beautiful, sparkly diamonds! For a long time, diamonds were rare. Because the supply was low, the price was high. Only the very rich could buy them. Then, in the 1870s, a big supply of diamonds was found in South Africa. This bigger supply made the price go down. Now many more people can buy diamonds.

Hands On: Buyers and Sellers

Often the supply and the demand of many items are not equal. Try this activity to see how sometimes the number of buyers is bigger or smaller than the number of things to buy.

What You Need

a group of friends
drawing paper
crayons, markers, or colored pencils

What You Do

1. Divide the group in half. One group is the buyers. The other group is the sellers.
2. Have each seller draw a picture of something to buy. They also write a number on their picture.
3. Ask each buyer to draw a picture of a person and write a number on the picture.
4. One seller holds up a picture. It might be a boat with the number 100. This means there are 100 boats for sale.
5. Then a buyer holds up a picture. It might be a person with the number 2,000. This means that there are 2,000 buyers.
6. Talk about the two pictures. Are there too many boats or not enough? Is the demand high or low? What will this do to the price? How could there be a balance?
7. Keep going until every buyer and seller has had a turn.

Glossary

amount (uh-MOUNT)—how much of something there is

balance (BAL-uhnss)—staying steady and not favoring one side or the other

choices (CHOYS-ez)—the things to pick from

customer (KUSS-tuh-mur)—someone who buys things from stores

goods (GUDZ)—real things a person can touch and use

price (PRISSE)—how much something costs

service (SUR-viss)—work that's done for other people

Read More

Berenstain, Stan, and Jan Berenstain. *The Berenstain Bears' Mad, Mad, Mad Toy Craze.* New York: Random House, 1999.

Godfrey, Neale S. *Neale S. Godfrey's Ultimate Kids' Money Book.* New York: Simon & Schuster, 1998.

Loewen, Nancy. *Lemons and Lemonade: A Book about Supply and Demand.* Minneapolis: Picture Window Books, 2004.

Internet Sites

FactHound offers a safe, fun way to find Internet sites related to this book. All of the sites on FactHound have been researched by our staff.

Here's how:
1. Visit *www.facthound.com*
2. Type in this special code **0736853979** for age-appropriate sites. Or enter a search word related to this book for a more general search.
3. Click on the **Fetch It** button.

FactHound will fetch the best sites for you!

Index